Count Pieri Nerli's study for the 1892 oil painting of Stevenson that appears on the front cover

KU-534-241

The Unique Author

Robert Louis Stevenson, as he has been known and loved for over a century (often simply as R. L. S.), was baptised Robert Lewis Balfour Stevenson. The only child of Thomas Stevenson and Margaret Isabella Balfour, he was born at 8 Howard Place, North Edinburgh on 13 November 1850.

Despite a lifelong struggle with a constitutional lung weakness, which he gallantly shrugged off as 'the wolverine on my shoulder', Stevenson achieved, not only in his lifetime the most prominent place in the world of English literature, but for all time a warm hold in the affections of readers in the Old and New Worlds. Like most other great writers, Stevenson waxes and wanes in popularity; but, like only a select few, it shall never be said of him, as has been remarked paradoxically of some classical writers, that the proof of his fame is that he is no longer read. As long as men and women are young at heart, as he always was, R. L. S. will delight them.

Enthusiasm for him reached a climax at the turn of the century. He was then subjected, both as a man and a writer, to a spate of harsh criticism which resulted in a slackening of popularity. One probable reaction to this was the formation of the Stevenson Club in 1920 in his native city. But the controversies were not entirely evil, for the revelations of the human dimensions of R. L. S. showed him to be not the 'seraph in chocolate' which some idolaters would have made him – though his best friends abhorred this image – but a flesh-and-blood hero.

Though Stevenson's narratives are popular, his fame does not depend entirely on these. He tried many forms of writing: moral, critical and personal essays, verse, short stories, argumentative articles and travel descriptions. He experimented with Gothic or horror stories, of which the most famous are *The Strange Case of Dr Jekyll and Mr Hyde* (the latter character a sort of Frankenstein's monster) and the *Suicide Club* series. Sensation seekers prefer these; others find his novels, especially *Treasure Island* and *Kidnapped*, more to their taste; while the charm of his essays or the beautiful simplicity and music of his verse appeal to many. The large extent of his writings in all these modes is not generally realised, nor is the wide variety and human interest of his many letters to all sorts of correspondents.

In short, Stevenson created a unique world in his brief and troubled life, powered by a brave and optimistic spirit that refused to surrender to continuous ill-health and other handicaps. He is, moreover, one of the few writers whose works cannot be dissociated from his personal charm.

Stevenson's mother, Margaret Isabella Stevenson, born at Colinton manse, twelfth and last child of the Rev. Lewis Balfour

Thomas Stevenson, father of Robert Louis, who hoped that his only son would follow in his footsteps as an illustrious civil engineer

Ancestral Heritage

The story of Stevenson is in many other respects one of the most remarkable in literature. His ancestry, though it is only a minor factor compared with his personality, yet helped in many ways to decide his character and actions.

On his mother's side he was descended from the Balfours of Pilrig, an estate between Edinburgh and Leith. They were a branch of a widely distributed Scottish family, distinguished in all fields. Margaret Isabella Balfour was a direct descendant of James Balfour of Pilrig (1703–95), who became a Sheriff-Substitute in Edinburgh. He was an eminent philosopher who had the temerity to argue with the famous historian and philosopher David Hume, who was generous enough to forgive him. Both his son and grandson were also distinguished scholars, so Stevenson's intellectual inheritance from his mother, quite apart from her angelic nature, was formidable. It is true that he also acquired from her a physical delicacy in the form of a lung weakness, but this was counterbalanced by her gift of humour and optimism.

In his father's family, going back only two generations, we find that the trait of mental stamina was even more illustrious. His paternal grandfather, from whom he got his first name, was the world-famous Robert Stevenson, who had succeeded his stepfather Thomas Smith as engineer to the Commission of Northern Lighthouses. For fifty years he designed and supervised the difficult building of many British lighthouses, the most famous of which was on the notorious Bell Rock off the mouth of the Tay, where hundreds of lives had been lost. Robert died in the year his grandson was born, but his three sons, Alan, David and Thomas, had continued the colossal task, and R. L. S.'s father was world-renowned for the building of harbours and lighthouses. As a matter of course he looked to his only child to follow the splendid family tradition.

Robert, however, apparently ignoring the dictates of love and duty, decided otherwise. Although his father's visions of a brilliant engineer were shattered by his son's obstinacy, he should have seen by this token that R. L. S. had inherited in full his paternal legacy of initiative and will power. His share of inventiveness was to be shown later. These gifts were not to be employed in combating the titanic forces of the ocean, or in contest with political or intellectual opponents, but in a much more influential way, by appealing to the emotions and reason of all mankind. Generous and wise though his father was in several aspects towards his wayward son, he took many years to realise that Robert, even in what appeared his gross folly, was wiser in the end.

Infancy

Despite his strength of will, Robert could not have triumphed entirely by his own efforts, enfeebled as he was by illnesses which led him into many crises, often barely avoiding death's door. He was loved and cosseted, indulged and pampered, to what seemed to insensitive persons an absurd degree, by his mother and his nurses, the most constant of whom was Alison Cunningham. A sturdy fisherman's daughter from Fife, thirty years of age, she entered her duties when her charge was eighteen months old. Coming of a simple religious family, she imbued the impressionable boy with biblical precepts, Calvinistic theology, psalm and hymn tunes and scripture history. Mingled with these was the hero-worship of the men and women of Covenanting persecution, the 'Killing Times' of the reign of Charles II. These early prejudices never left Stevenson's mental background, but with this rather narrow approach to life were interwoven romantic tales and ballads of the sea, of smugglers, pirates and treasure trove, of witches and the supernatural, in which the coast of Fife was rich. These made some compensation for the terrors of the Calvinist world of vengeful Jehovahs and everlasting torments. 'Cummy' was described later in Stevenson's life (for he never failed to be grateful to her) as his 'first wife'. She lived twenty years after her famous charge, retaining fond memories of him into extreme old age.

The Bell Rock Lighthouse, built by R. L. S.'s grandfather. The painting, by A. Macdonald, 1820, was later presented to Alison Cunningham, R. L. S.'s nurse. The rock on which the lighthouse is built had caused hundreds of shipwrecks even though a warning bell was fixed on it. This rock being tidal, work on it could only be intermittent and all the stonework was prefabricated on the mainland at Arbroath

Alison Cunningham (1822-1913). Stevenson's childhood nurse, 'Cummy', whom he described as 'My second mother, my first wife, the angel of my infant life', outlived him by twenty years. Painted by Fiddes Watt in 1908

3

Stevenson at four years of age; the charm
that inspired such devotion in his nurse and
mother is plain to see

At six, Stevenson's distinctive facial features
are already well formed as he poses for the
camera with precocious assurance

Nevertheless, these indulgences, which would have been unobtainable by an impoverished child, who would undoubtedly have perished in infancy, were not whimsically bestowed on 'the smout', as his mother humorously nicknamed him. In all his childish troubles he never showed the least signs of being peevish or spoilt. He repaid the thousand tendernesses of his young mother and foster mother with quaint and humorous little sayings and actions. He even dictated a *History of Moses* to his nurse when he was five, not yet writing. The ever-present threat of the death of their only hope merely intensified their affection, and redoubled it after his unexpected recovery from a severe gastric fever in his eighth year. Both his father and mother, following the familiar domestic habits of that age, had been of a family of twelve, so it almost seemed that the love which might have been spread over a large family was concentrated upon a solitary child.

Schooling and Early Environment

Although J. H. Miller, in his *History of Scottish Literature*, 1903, unfeelingly wrote that 'the discipline of a long course at a good public school was the sovereign specific for the only child', he had to acknowledge that school for Stevenson was quite out of the question. Until Robert was seven he did not attend school and read very haltingly. There is, however, a tradition that before he was seven he tried to enrol at the local board school at Canonmills but he was so ill-treated on account of his genteel appearance that he fled in terror and never returned. At that time schooling was not yet compulsory, though, as the fees were nominal, most parents sent their children. The Stevensons agreed that a private school would be best, at least for a start, so Robert was enrolled with Mr Henderson, who ran a small tutorial school for boys in India Street, not far from the new home at 17 Heriot Row.

It would be as well at this point to describe the various houses the family had inhabited in the area. When first married in 1848, Margaret and Thomas resided in

No. 8 Howard Place, birthplace of R. L. S.   No. 17 Heriot Row

Howard Place, really a part of the long Inverleith Row extending north from Canonmills Bridge over the Water of Leith to Goldenacre on the Leith boundary. When Robert was three they moved to Inverleith Terrace – not a good choice, for it was a cold damp house with a northern aspect. In 1857, after suffering four years of discomfort, they moved to Heriot Row, halfway up the long slope towards Princes Street. It was a terraced house in a very elegant area of the New Town, facing south with access by rented key to extensive private gardens with great forest trees of elm, horse-chestnut and ash, gravelled paths, lawns and birdsong.

In fact the district of North Edinburgh where Stevenson spent his formative years was, from the middle to the end of the last century, a pleasant *rus in urbe*, that is, it was near the city, but consisted of farmland, private gardens, nurseries and parks. Like all the countryside around Edinburgh it was dotted with little properties and quaint mansion houses belonging to well-established families. When Stevenson was a boy the public could enjoy the magnificent Botanic Gardens, a piece of undulating woodland of over thirty acres, which had formerly been the estate belonging to Inverleith Mansion-house. It was a short distance from Howard Place. Not far off to the east the estate of Warriston had recently been taken over by a company as a cemetery. There, with a splendid panoramic view of Edinburgh, lie many of the illustrious poets, writers, artists, scholars, divines and warriors of Victorian Scotland. In both of these totally dissimilar enclosures Cummy and her small charge wandered, probably mingling on the Sabbath with the many family parties who promenaded in that era to the 'Botanics', or to one of the many well-ordered graveyards, on a day when reading was restricted to religious books and tombstones. In a letter, long after and far away, Stevenson revealed that the line in the twenty-third psalm, 'Yea, though I walk in death's dark vale,' always recalled his childhood's dread of walking along a hollow road amongst the Warriston graves.

5

Edinburgh from Warriston Cemetery, a place that left a lifelong impression on the young writer (from *Old and New Edinburgh,* 1883)

Mr Henderson's school was a happy place, though Robert's attendance there was interrupted by illness. In 1860, however, he was deemed to be fit enough, and well enough grounded in the elements, to face the rough and tumble of the classrooms and playground of the Edinburgh Academy, one of the three Classical Schools of Edinburgh, priding itself as much on Greek as on Latin, with many other subjects. But Robert's attendance for eighteen months was only perfunctory, broken by illness and disinclination. He then, for a spell, enrolled at Mr Thomson's small school in nearby Frederick Street and, on visiting the south of England for his health in the autumn of 1863, he attended Mr Wyatt's boarding school in London.

On return to Edinburgh he was tutored at home by his old teacher Mr Henderson, who held him in high esteem as an apt scholar.

Edinburgh Academy (from *Old and New Edinburgh,* 1883)

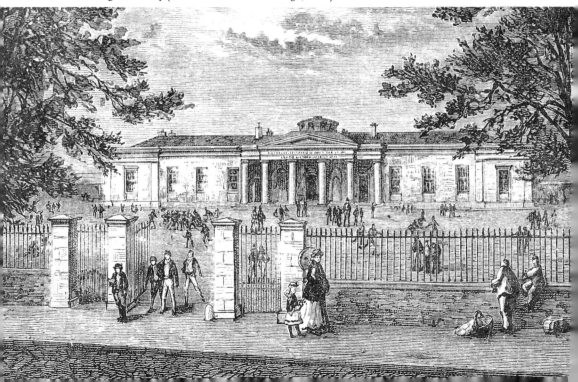

colour
I don't know the date

The manse at Colinton, where R. L. S. often played until the age of ten, when his grandfather, the Rev. Lewis Balfour, died

Extract from a characteristically humorous letter by the youthful R. L. S. to his cousin Henrietta Traquair

> My dear Cat I am at present watching other people taking tea and hear Willie saying in a doleful tone, "I don't know what to say". But as I am in the same state I can not afford to laugh at him Momma says you wish to know what is going on so here goes— Mr Traquair is reading the newspaper, Jessie is clearing away the tea things, Uncle Ramsay is looking at the cattle, and the rest are all writing to a certain person called puss. Pray tell me whether Rosa Lind is a

Early Preparations for Authorship

Long before adolescence Stevenson had implicitly decided on a literary career, as could have been foreshadowed by his infantile *History of Moses*. When he was nine, on holiday, he composed *Travels in Perth*, and at thirteen he wrote a satire on the inhabitants of Peebles on the lines of Thackeray's *Book of Snobs*, which even at that age was his favourite reading, along with *Rob Roy* by Scott. The following year he wrote a libretto in comic vein, *The Baneful Potato*. When nearly sixteen, well familiar with the Pentland Hills, only a short walk from the Colinton manse of his mother's father, the Rev. Lewis Balfour, he published his first book, privately and anonymously. It was a small pamphlet on the Pentland Rising of 1666, when the Westland Covenanters were suppressed with much brutality at Rullion Green, only four miles from Swanston Cottage, which the Stevensons rented the following year. The booklet was sold for a few shillings to those who were interested, but it was almost immediately withdrawn from circulation by his father. Copies were soon so rare as to be almost unobtainable. Even before Stevenson's death they fetched £12 each. The book consists mainly of extracts from Covenanting writers of the 'Killing Times' (1660–88), or from Wodrow a few years later. But the linking parts by the schoolboy author, newly sixteen when it was published (to coincide with the bicentenary of the battle, on 28 November 1866), are expressed with admirable literacy.

During his boyhood and adolescence he built up the immeasurably varied impressions of background which were to be utilised in his later writings. The Old Town of Edinburgh still retained much of its ancient character, which Stevenson describes as Gothic, its rudeness merely emphasised by the more recent accessions of contrasting Greek architecture in various imitated classical styles, both in housing and more imposing monuments and public buildings.

R. L. S. at sixteen, when *Pentland Rising* was published

Swanston Cottage, in the Pentland Hills, as painted by Robert Hope

In his book of extraordinarily perceptive pictures, entitled *Edinburgh: Picturesque Notes*, he shows his love-hate attitude to his mother city. He spares no harsh realism, neither does he conceal his deep affection for 'Auld Reekie', that harridan who would have immolated her delicate offspring had he remained under her capricious skies. His ironic references to the douce or respectable inhabitants of the New Town, as represented perhaps by his own parents, drew forth many protests from those who were caricatured, which only shows the justice of the criticism. His chief objections to the Edinburgh gentry lay in their display of 'Churchianity' – Sabbatarianism, snobbery and narrow pessimism.

But his real heart was with the upland solitudes so close to the city, especially his beloved Pentland Hills in whose bosom Swanston Cottage was cradled – really a commodious two-storeyed villa, owned by the Town Council. It was a fine centre from which to explore all the hills and valleys within a day's journey. Even at the end of his life, from Samoa, he penned the most exquisitely touching picture of the

Rullion Green, site of the heroic stand of the Westland Covenanters which inspired Stevenson's first published work; in the distance, his beloved Pentland Hills

Pentlands, in his poem to the novelist S. R. Crockett. As a young man he engaged in conversation with the few denizens of the hills, mostly shepherds. Such a one was John Todd, the 'roaring shepherd' of Swanston, who actually set his dogs on Stevenson because he was accompanied by his own pet dog, Coolin, named after the Skye mountains. But the charm of the city boy won the gruff old shepherd's heart.

The memorial at Rullion Green to the two ministers slain by the dragoons, with fifty of their flock, was a mecca for the young author. And he also haunted, as he says in a letter from Samoa, and will ever haunt in ghostly form, the ruins of the Auld Kirk of Glencorse, on its wooded knoll half-encompassed by the Glencorse Burn. There are buried many of the French prisoners-of-war, who feature in his novel *St Ives*, a romance of Napoleonic times.

Beyond the Pentlands he also in boyhood frequented the other upland wildernesses, almost as unpopulated as the remotest Highlands. These were the Moorfoot, Lammermoor and Meldon Hills and Peeblesshire Heights, 'hills of sheep, and the howes of the silent vanished races', of mountain hares, grouse, whaups and peewees (curlews and lapwings).

This countryside forms the setting of much of *Weir of Hermiston*, written vividly from ten thousand miles away.

His visits farther afield, to Fife fishing villages, to the West Highlands and the Ayrshire coast, especially of Carrick, the scene of *The Master of Ballantrae*, were laying the foundations for his novels. In his long vacations and visits to London and Bournemouth he imbibed the atmosphere of the early part of *Treasure Island*, of *Dr Jekyll and Mr Hyde* and the *New Arabian Nights*. For R. L. S. the scene was absolutely paramount to the sentiment of the story. Even in the tense horror of 'Jekyll and Hyde' he slackens the pace over a long paragraph to describe in detail the autumn scene in a London suburb.

John Todd, Pentland Shepherd, from the Pentland
Essays, illustrated by Robert Hope

The Auld Kirk of Glencorse, now in ruins,
is lost in the woods above the Glencorse Burn

Influences on Style

In all these wanderings, though he sometimes enjoyed companionship, Stevenson's preference was for solitude. But he was not a 'loner'. In its proper place he loved society, with a small 's'; he lived to study the manners and minds of mankind – though he confessed to his inability to comprehend women, with a few notable exceptions.

Despite this great accumulation of impressions, he realised early that these would have been quite inert for his life purpose unless incorporated in a style, or rather a large repertoire of styles, that could adequately present his material. To achieve mastery of English and, to a complementary degree, of Scots, was the labour of long years. This necessarily entailed partial successes, even total failures; but none of these were wasted, because they all proved in his case to be steps towards perfection. This progress in writing was by no means consistent. He had remarkable, but not undeserved, successes with the public quite early on; then after some disappointments he sailed with the high tide of popular favour.

He tells us, in frank confession, of the imitations he made of former authors who attracted him. He 'played the sedulous ape' to certain quaint, highly individualistic, not to say eccentric, writers. In English, while he did not dispute the pervading excellence of the Bible, of Shakespeare and of Bunyan, he was engrossed with Sir Thomas Browne, Hobbes and Sir Thomas Urquhart, the Scot who wrote in superbly masterful English. In French, a tongue which Stevenson early acquired in full, his model of prose was Montaigne's Essays; in Spanish, in several English translations, Cervantes's *Don Quixote*.

Perhaps as influential on his style was William Hazlitt the elder, the English essayist of the early nineteenth century, who was seen by Stevenson as a splendid writer to copy, very close to his heart. Of him he said in *Virginibus Puerisque*, 'though we are mighty fine fellows nowadays, we cannot write like Hazlitt'.

In poetry Stevenson perhaps thought of himself as one of a triumvirate: these were the three Roberts – Burns, Fergusson and himself. Although he expressed in print his disapproval of the moral behaviour of the other two, which displeased their admirers, he was much influenced by their poetry, especially in Scots, though all three were also masters of classical English. Of the French poets he took as his hero the Parisian bohemian and housebreaker François Villon, to whom, despite his scandalous character, the bourgeois Stevenson extended a fraternal handshake across the centuries.

The French influence, very pervasive in Stevenson's whole lifetime, was however not beneficial, especially to his prose. During his formative years in literature a wide pedantic movement affected European literature, the cult of realism, combined with the technique of *le mot juste*, or the fitting word. This led to a preciousness in writing and an off-putting 'smell of the lamp'. Gustave Flaubert, author of the scandalous *Madame Bovary* (which would not raise a modern eyebrow), was the leader. Stevenson, after dallying with this school, managed to expel himself before damaging his style, though traces of it do not enhance his early works.

With the ambition to write as well as these geniuses of varied colours, it is no wonder that Stevenson was sometimes judged to be foolishly ambitious. But the truth is that the mass of the reading public was purblind to the uniqueness of such a writer in a prosaic age. He was a true romantic, imbued with a resurrection of the Gothic spirit, of the fantastic, the grotesque, the horrible. His art at its best was fascinating, even irresistible. He was therefore very sensitive to the malicious sneers by ignoramuses which he encountered personally or in print. At Grèz–sur–Loing, in company at dinner, an impudent young Irish artist of no ability introduced Stevenson publicly as a 'Scotch literary mediocrity'. He was stung to the quick, says his stepson Lloyd Osbourne, and he resented that double insult all his life, for the attribute 'Scotch' was a sneer to imply that he had little aptitude for the English language.

Two Careers Abandoned

Over and above his early literary apprenticeship, Stevenson studied for his father's profession, civil engineering, at Edinburgh University, where he published some articles in the *Student* magazine between 1868 and 1871. He was so successful in the engineering class that he was awarded the Silver Medal of the Edinburgh Society of Arts for his paper on lighthouse improvements, which probably owed something to his father's advice. All seemed set for the brilliant career of Robert L. B. Stevenson, civil engineer. He had even acquired some practical experience of the sea, and of lighthouse and harbour construction, at Anstruther, Fife, at Wick in Caithness, and at the Dhu Heartach Lighthouse, then being built in the Hebrides off the coast of Mull. At these places he stored vivid memories for his writing.

In 1871 came the bombshell. In a stormy scene he told his father that he was not going forward as his successor. Thomas Stevenson was not a man to be approached lightly. His portrait has been drawn for us by his son in a semi-fictitious publication, *The Misadventures of John Nicholson*, showing the strange nature of his father – a man of extremes, stern yet kind, melancholy yet genial, chivalrous but with many faults of insensitivity. Such was Robert's determination that his father

Cunzie House, Anstruther. This is where R. L. S. lodged in 1868 when he was engaged in practical civil engineering with his father, who was at that time constructing the harbour extension at Anstruther

Parliament House, Edinburgh, originally built about 1640 to house the Scottish Parliament. Inside is the magnificent Parliament Hall where it has long been the custom for lawyers to perambulate as R. L. S. did during his brief spell

saw it was useless to pursue the matter; he therefore compromised and suggested a suitable alternative in a city that had long been the stronghold of the law. So Robert took up a legal course in the University of Edinburgh and after four years, during which time he was able to divert himself in the long vacations with writing, reading and congenial companionship, he was called to the bar.

But although being offered two causes to plead, when he might well have paced Parliament Hall for years in vain, he refused both, and never attempted a practice. His appearance was said to be so unbecoming to judicial dignity that he was ridiculed by his colleagues.

Rebellion

Robert was, however, indifferent to the scorn of his peers, for these legal years had not been entirely eaten by the locusts. He was gaining experience of life and, as is normal, paying dearly for such wisdom as he acquired. He observes in *Kidnapped* that both fools and knaves eventually are punished in this world, but the fools first. Some critics say that he merely sought friendship and adventure in order to write about them, but this is plainly not true. He also sought human relationship, and ups and downs of life, for their own sakes, and often wished he had not. As things turned out, all these brushes with reality helped him to develop a muscular trenchant style (but which he perfected only when it was too late; when he died the world was left to regret a great promise only partly fulfilled). In his personal relations, too, he was often imposed upon, but chivalrously he never complained.

Bull's Close by J. Stewart Smith. A typical scene in the Old Town which R. L. S. frequented in his 'Velvet Jacket' days as a student

Stevenson at the rebellious age of twenty, wearing the black coat that earned him the sobriquet 'Velvet Jacket' in the taverns

This personal life, apart from his two professional lives, repays studying at the period of his emergence into manhood, from 1868, for it bears heavily on his achievements. As with most young folk it was a phase of rebellion against conventions, represented by the father or mother figure, or both. He extended his dissent so far as to announce to his parents that he no longer believed in God, which of course implied that he would not be bound by the Presbyterian tenets or the Ten Commandments. This declaration caused anguish and bitter recriminations which drove all three to despair, especially when Robert revealed that he belonged to a freethinkers' club, which included his older cousin the talented R. A. M. Stevenson. Thomas Stevenson did not help matters when he openly accosted his nephew in the street and accused him of leading Robert into agnosticism and hellfire.

Edinburgh, in Victorian times, despite its reputation for sanctity, was a very suitable place for going to the dogs, and Stevenson had no lack of companions to share his revolt, though many of them had never known any moral restraint. Such an accusation of lack of principles could never be laid at Stevenson's door. Whether he kept the moral code or broke it, he was always keenly aware of it. In fact it was said, in summing up his character, that he was in essence a Presbyterian preacher. He may have made half-hearted attempts to break away from the moral law but he never was successful. In fact, in 'Jekyll and Hyde' and one or two similar tales the prevailing note is almost pure moral allegory. They were expounded as such from the contemporary pulpits of Britain.

Although conjectures and allegations have been made, not much is known for certain about Stevenson's 'Mr Hyde' period in the Old Town. It was, as we have indicated, never possible for him to emulate the extremes of his created monster, but he must have witnessed some depraved characters in the Cowgate dens, where even the police dared not venture unless in a posse. R. L. S. was nicknamed 'Velvet Jacket' in the demi-monde, because of the expensive black jacket his father had given him. He has been accused, by those who set themselves up to be judges in Israel, of fatuous Bohemianism – of being a poseur, adopting fads and committing sins for show. If he did, he was not alone, for the Edinburgh students of that time were a much wilder bunch than would have been expected, coming as many of them did from the well-fenced kailyards of the Scottish rural scene. But they were little different from students of all ages, and a constant war of attrition was waged between 'Toun and Goun' in which the police were often involved in quelling riots caused by high spirits.

A horse-drawn tram of the type that Kate Drummond may have ridden into the city to meet R. L. S.

A medieval proverb probably known to R. L. S. is,

Qui hante femmes et dez
Il mourra en pauvretez.

(He who frequents women and dice will die in poverty).

Luckily or unluckily for Stevenson such a fate was never likely to be his, not only because his family was wealthy, but for the stronger reason that his father, arguing from false premises, decided that by severely restricting his son's allowance he would prevent him from indulging such vices as he had. Paradoxically, then, he lived in poverty. He was allowed only half-a-crown or a crown weekly, which cannot be put down to miserliness on his father's part, for he provided very generous entertainment for Robert's friends when they were invited to 17 Heriot Row. But this sparse allowance for a youth of eighteen in a well-to-do family had the opposite effect to that intended. 'Velvet Jacket' was driven by this parsimony to the cheapest pleasure resorts, where only his charming manners and amusing conversation prevented him from being bounced out when his money ran short. The Leith and Old Town *filles de joie* were very pleased to pay for his drink until next allowance day.

About this time he fell in love with Kate Drummond, daughter of the Highland blacksmith at Swanston. With other country lads and lasses she probably walked part of the way to Edinburgh and then took the horse tram from Church Hill to the city centre. She was a frank, active, well-built lass of his own age with no genteel Edinburgh prudery. She bore a name distinguished in Scottish history. Stevenson wanted to marry her though he had no income, and he boldly put the proposition to his shocked father, who utterly refused to pay one penny towards such a misalliance. Another family crisis proved too much for his affection. He promised to give her up but, as he admitted later, he thought the worse of himself for his surrender. The image of Kate lingered all his life, and her rather earthy but otherwise admirable womanhood has been traced in two of his successful heroines, the younger Kirsty Elliot in *Weir of Hermiston* and Barbara Grant in *Catriona*.

Another acquaintance of his late teens was Mary of Leith, surname not revealed. He was much taken by her frank kindness and may well have applied Shelley's lines to their brief friendship:

Yield love for love, warm, frank and true,
As Burns the Scottish peasant boy
Knew better far than you.

Along with Highland Kate he cherished the memory of this bonny lassie, but anyone familiar with the Great Divide of Edinburgh snobbery, in Victorian and later times, sympathises with the heartaches these renunciations must have caused the highly sensitive boy.

It was about this time that he decided to change his name. Henceforth he was to be called Robert Louis Stevenson, effecting two changes. The Balfour was to be dropped altogether, perhaps because the full name was too cumbersome, for he had no quarrel with his mother's people. Indeed he continued to owe a great deal to them and was often with his many Balfour cousins at the Colinton manse. The spelling of Lewis was changed at his father's insistence, because, as a staunch Tory, he had taken umbrage at a Radical councillor named Lewis. The pronunciation remained, however, and Louis was not pronounced in the French style. To his nearest and dearest he was simply Lou.

Matrimonial Entanglements

During his final years as a law student Louis travelled extensively in Europe, mostly in his beloved France. The winter of 1873–74, as much for his mother's health as for his own, was spent at Mentone, where he began many ambitious projects, including a romance based on the life of the Covenanting zealot, the Fife laird, Hackston of Rathillet. But, as with Burns, if any work displeased him, he flung it into the fire. These visits to France were to have the greatest effect on his personal life, as also were the many friendships he made in London, where he was a member of the Savile Club, much frequented by artists and writers, many of whom, including Andrew Lang, George Meredith and Sidney Colvin, were his close friends. His brilliant cousin, R. A. M. Stevenson of the former freethinkers' club, was a noted artist. He introduced Louis to the international community at Barbizon, in the lovely countryside about seventy miles south of Paris, in the midst of the great forest of Fontainebleau.

Siron's Inn, Barbizon, on the edge of the forest of Fontainebleu. Stevenson stayed here in 1875, referring to it as 'that excellent artists' barrack'

R. L. S. at twenty-five - about the time he fell in love with Fanny Osbourne

This portrait of Fanny Osbourne, taken at about the time of her first meeting with Stevenson, depicts a masterful and unpredictable character capable of devoted love but also of violent and unreasonable fits of frustration and jealousy

Here he met an American lady, a friend of his cousin. She was separated from her husband and was accompanied by her son and daughter. Louis immediately fell in love with her. Her maiden name had been Frances (or Fanny) Matilda Van de Grift, of old pioneer stock, mixed Dutch and Swedish. She was dark and vivacious. She had been married at seventeen to Samuel Osbourne, of twenty, who turned out to be dissolute and unfaithful. Consequently Fanny had known the harshness of life, in the mining camps of the West, and had recently, in France, sat by the deathbed of a beloved son of four. At thirty-five she welcomed the friendship of the lively and talented young Scot, ten years younger. Her son Lloyd and daughter Isobel, or Belle, also liked him.

Although Stevenson, to the end of his life, maintained that Fanny was the one woman in all the world for him, it has often been a cause for surprise that he should have chosen such a masterful and temperamental mate. The Swedes and the Dutch are not the phlegmatic folk generally supposed, and the mixture was often highly unstable, as in Fanny's case. Probably Stevenson inspired an overwhelming pity in her.

After their marriage in 1880, they appeared almost reconciled to the tragic probability that he would survive only a few months. But she nursed, mothered and sweethearted him to such good effect that he lived another fourteen years.

There is, however, another factor which on his side possibly created a fatal passion for Mrs Osbourne. A year or two before his acquaintance with Fanny

Osbourne he had met, in the Savile Club in London, one of the most attractive women in that circle. She was Mrs Sitwell, née Frances (or Fanny) Jane Featherstonehaugh, of an old Irish landed family. By a strange but not unconnected multiple coincidence, this other Fanny was also ten years his senior and had also been married at seventeen; she too had separated herself from a dissolute husband, a clergyman. She also had had a family, one of whom had died young. But there was a radical difference between the two namesakes. Mrs Sitwell was deeply in love with Sidney Colvin, head of the Slade School of Art, a rigidly moral man, whose matrimonial principles were those of his age. His associations with Mrs Sitwell were beyond reproach, as events were to prove: he waited until the death of the Rev. Mr Sitwell, early in the twentieth century, before he married the now elderly widow, by which time he had been knighted and she became Lady Colvin.

Stevenson had fallen in love on sight, as who had not, with the voluptuous Fanny Sitwell. But the three-year affair never got beyond a kind of Platonic friendship in actuality. The sexual relationship was sublimated in letters of such intensity, on Stevenson's part at any rate, that they are still held in a cedarwood box by the Keeper of MSS in the National Library of Scotland. But Louis, at her insistent request, burnt all her love letters so that no scandal should ever reach the ears of Sidney Colvin.

It is a strange story, incredible to our generation, but it helps to explain Stevenson's attraction to Fanny Osbourne, especially as, unlike Mrs Sitwell, she yielded to his pleadings and became his mistress, though this established fact was vehemently denied by her family after the death of R. L. S. and her own demise.

Literary Success and Marriage

During the seventies Stevenson was becoming known to a limited circle for several brilliant articles in London magazines, especially the *Cornhill Magazine*, always favourably disposed to his skilful work. Some of these were later to be published in book form in collections known as *Virginibus Puerisque* and *Familiar Studies of Men and Books*. The first title is a quotation from an ode of Horace beginning, 'I hate the vulgar crowd, I sing to youths and maidens.'

The record of a canoe trip through Belgium and Northern France in 1876 with his friend Sir Walter Simpson, son of the inventor of the use of chloroform, was published as *An Inland Voyage* in 1878 and immediately established Stevenson in literary circles.

1878 was a year of furious invention and resulted in the publication in 1879 of *Travels with a Donkey in the Cévennes* and in 1882 of the *New Arabian Nights*. The first was a fascinating account of a romantic hike through the sequestered forest country of central France, with unforgettable word pictures of Stevenson sleeping out in the lonely forest glades, with Modestine, the strong-willed donkey, tethered nearby; the second was a collection of macabre short stories based in London.

Despite his increasing reputation Stevenson was very upset when Mrs Osbourne decided in 1878 to return to America with her family. After an anxious and uncertain few months he was relieved to get a cable from Fanny inviting him to join her. With a precipitancy that astonished and alarmed his friends, who considered his condition very frail, he set off secretly on a very hazardous expedition from which he was fortunate to escape alive. He describes his traumatic experiences fully in literature and letters. Although the horrors and privations of a steerage emigrant were alleviated for him by the use of a private cabin, he was still very debilitated in body and mind on disembarking. Then came the weary train journey

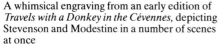

A whimsical engraving from an early edition of *Travels with a Donkey in the Cévennes,* depicting Stevenson and Modestine in a number of scenes at once

Frontispiece, drawn by Belle Osbourne, of the first edition of *The Silverado Squatters,* showing her mother and Louis in the abandoned mine buildings where they began their married life

across the prairies, and the hardships in the backwoods, where he was miraculously saved from death, when found seriously ill, by two pioneers.

But it all seemed worthwhile when Fanny, through the less strict American laws, had secured the divorce impossible for British citizens. They were married in California in 1880 and, even in the primitive hardships of a deserted shack, found a sort of paradise, described in 1883 in *The Silverado Squatters.*

Braving parental disapproval the Stevensons returned to Edinburgh where, surprisingly, they were warmly welcomed at Heriot Row and given not only a blessing but the more-needed financial backing. Thomas Stevenson approved of Fanny to the extent of later recommending his son never to publish anything unless it had her approval. As we shall see, this principle was not always reliable.

Although Louis's fortunes were decidedly on the mend, his health did not permit him to remain in Britain, so the newly-weds went to Davos, a health resort in the Swiss Alps. The bracing air inspired Stevenson to the finalisation of *Virginibus Puerisque* and the brilliant assemblage of critical essays, *Familiar Studies of Men and Books.* Out of his memories of diablerie, told him by Cummy, he also composed the tale of a Scottish witch, *Thrawn Janet,* written in Scots. He admits that he scared himself in the composition of it. But all these were completely overshadowed by a story originally entitled *The Sea Cook,* later changed to *Treasure Island.*

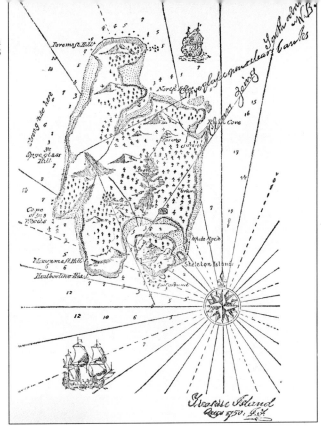

Map of Treasure Island taken
from an edition of 1923

Inspired by a fictitious map drawn by his stepson Lloyd while the family visited Deeside in Scotland, *Treasure Island* was at first only a serialised story, poorly printed on the coarsest of paper for juvenile readers, but it swept into favour with all readers, of whatever age. The style, an imitation of eighteenth-century narrative, puts the work into a classical category along with *Robinson Crusoe*. The only weakness is an interruption in the narrative when Jim Hawkins's tale is taken over briefly by Dr Livesey for three chapters. As in the later *Kidnapped*, the hero is not the story-teller; he is the picaresque John Silver, the sea-cook, of equivocal character, a one-legged intelligent man based on Stevenson's friend William Ernest Henley, a Gloucester-born poet and writer, who had suffered amputation for tuberculosis, and whose ambivalence of character made him a good model for Long John Silver. Stevenson had first met him in the Royal Infirmary of Edinburgh and decided to immortalise him.

An illustration of a scene in
Treasure Island which appeared in
Young Folks magazine in 1881

Residence at Bournemouth

Three years, mostly in Europe, failed to restore Stevenson's health, though it helped him financially and in reputation. Bournemouth seemed a suitable residence, on the mild sunny Channel coast, so the family took over a villa there from July 1884 until August 1887. The house was congenially named Skerryvore after one of the Stevenson lighthouses, designed by Uncle Alan and built in partnership with Louis's father. Much of the stay at Bournemouth was spent in work that was to prove unprofitable. Stevenson collaborated with Henley in several plays which were not conspicuously successful; indeed Stevenson was best working alone. *Prince Otto*, a romance in which he seriously tried to create credible women, though a masterpiece of style which took him two precious years, was a form he never repeated. But he scored a new and unexpected triumph in the celebrated *A Child's Garden of Verses*, which broke new ground in its approach to writing for children by refusing to accept the centuries-long belief that they were really adults in miniature. Although this collection has lost much of its former appeal, it won the hearts of two generations of adults and a score of generations of children.

The title page from *A Child's Garden of Verses,* which was published in 1885 and achieved great popularity

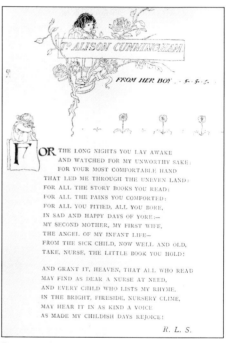

Poem 'To Alison Cunningham from Her Boy', from *A Child's Garden of Verses*

Immediately, to the puzzlement, shock and scandal of the British public, appeared the very antithesis of bland verses, *The Strange Case of Dr Jekyll and Mr Hyde*. The theme was dual personality, a condition not then generally familiar to the public, and one which Stevenson had previously treated in a short story, *Markheim*. Although the author did not personally intervene with moral comments, but merely described the case from several viewpoints, the publication of 'Jekyll and Hyde' caused a furore incredible to our generation. Such was the effect of a Gothic tale of horror, a form resurrected by Stevenson from a century before, anticipating the Romantic revival. No wonder the author is rightly credited with inventing two of the most evocative names in literature.

Stevenson at thirty-five in genial mood, perhaps as a result of his growing literary success

'Skerryvore', Bournemouth, bought for Fanny as a wedding present by Louis's father, is shown here in a 1912 engraving. The house was destroyed in the Second World War, but the layout is preserved in a public garden

The strange part of the story is that the idea came to Stevenson in a nightmare or, as he puts it, 'from the goblins'. It was so shocking that he cried out, and was awakened by Fanny to reveal what had alarmed him. He straightaway committed the story to paper, but when he read the first draft to Fanny she was so disgusted that, to his livid fury, she severely censured the whole idea and he destroyed it. Luckily for future generations he uncharacteristically defied her, and incidentally his father's advice, and rewrote it in an even more emphatic and artistic form. Although such a master stroke is unusual, though not unique in his works, it reinforced his reputation and brought a handsome return for only three days' writing; though, to be just, it was really the result of many years of philosophising on the conflicting aspects of personality.

The small boy who loved to arrange the furniture to form a pulpit and pews, and who insisted on being the minister to the extent of wearing a paper dog collar, was the same at heart as the moralist who created Jekyll and Hyde.

At Bournemouth a new source of material was tapped which finally established Stevenson as a leading novelist. As is well known, Sir Walter Scott chivalrously killed himself with overwork on the vast series of the Waverley novels and other books, written into the night in the last eighteen years of his life. Although Scott seemed to have exhausted the romance of Scottish history, Stevenson had a passion to revive it. He was well read in it, and he found an unworked patch in the political and criminal trials of the mid–eighteenth century, and particularly in the ancient clan rivalries of the Campbells and the Stewarts, still persisting after the suppressions following Culloden. The highlight of this period was the murder of Colin Campbell of Glenure, the 'Red Fox', followed by the patently unjust execution of James Stewart for a crime he did not commit.

In *Kidnapped*, published in 1886, Stevenson introduced his mother's family in David Balfour but, like Jim Hawkins in *Treasure Island*, only as a witness. We are led on a stirring adventure, told again in imitation of eighteenth-century prose, through the Highlands and Lowlands of Scotland in 1751. It entails family intrigue, kidnapping, shipwreck, manhunt and murder. The reader could hardly ask for more, unless a love interest, which is absent.

Stevenson explains that the story is not intended to be historically exact. He knew the facts from his study of the recorded trials and from James Stewart's gallows-foot statement of innocence. But the essentials of colourful background came from his own memories. He invented David Balfour, and went to work on the raw material of the Gaelic-speaking, tall, emaciated desperado, Alan Breck Stewart, to turn him into the attractive hero, innocent of the murder of which the real Alan Breck would certainly have been found guilty had he not been so slippery. A longer complete book was intended, enabling all the loose ends to be tied up happily. On consideration Stevenson ended *Kidnapped* with David's coming into his inheritance. The sequel, *Catriona*, published in 1893, though brilliantly written, and with the author's best portrayal of women characters, does not have the dramatic appeal of the fast-moving *Kidnapped*.

Edinburgh from 'Rest and be Thankful', a humorous name given to the summit of Corstorphine Hill, Edinburgh, where travellers could sit and view the city. Here, in *Kidnapped*, the story ends by David and Alan Breck parting, David going to the city to claim his fortune (from *Old and New Edinburgh*, 1883)

Final Departure from Britain

Although several more works, including *Memories and Portraits* and *Underwoods*, a fine collection of general poetry, were written at Skerryvore, the Bournemouth period came to an end in 1887, when the decisive point in Stevenson's life was reached: he lay seriously ill with lung trouble for several weeks, totally prostrated. He had been working too hard and the culminating blow came in the midst of his labour, early in May 1887. Word came from Edinburgh that his father was *in extremis*. Louis arrived too late to speak to him and was left with the melancholy duty of posting funeral notices. In the autumn, after his convalescence, the family

17 Heriot Row,
Edinburgh, 10th May 1887

Sir,

The favor of your Company to attend the Funeral of my Father, from his house here, to the place of Interment in the New Calton Burying Ground, on Friday the 13th Curt at ½ past 2 o'clock, will much oblige,

Sir,

Your obedient Servant,

Robert Louis Stevenson

Request from Stevenson to attend his father's funeral, dated 10 May 1887

set off by steamship for the USA, where they took a lodge in the pure air of the Adirondack Mountains, in north-west New York State. Here, at an altitude of nearly two thousand feet, in the Great Northern Wilderness of six thousand square miles of woodland, lake, river and peak, they wintered in the frosty but dry air. In the spring of 1888 they were again on the move to the coast of New Jersey, but even here the climate proved uncongenial, and summer found them in San Francisco, with the handicap of sea fogs. Now determined to continue the search for a salubrious paradise, on 26 June 1888, through an agent, Stevenson commissioned the yacht *Casco* to sail as fancy dictated through the vast emptiness of the Central Pacific. The expenses were to be met by a weekly travelogue in letter form in the New York *World*, arranged by the McClure Syndicate, which published thirty-four letters in all before going on strike. McClure was a literary impresario. Fifteen letters, not used by McClure, were later printed privately under the title *South Seas: A Record of Three Cruises*. These, and a further twenty, were included in the Edinburgh edition of Stevenson's works, entitled *In the South Seas*. This was published separately in 1900 by Chatto and Windus. Such a prescribed form of writing was not to his taste, but Louis persisted in it whenever he felt fit, or in the mood. The dollar stood at five to the pound in those days, but the $2000 fee bought a lot in Oceania.

The house in the Adirondack Mountains where the Stevenson family spent the winter of 1887-88

Casco, the yacht that was the Stevensons' home for a year

Samoa

One of Stevenson's most evocative lines is 'blue days at sea'. These idyllic years realised this: they were his happiest though not the most productive of literature. For six months the Stevensons stayed at Honolulu and were charmed by the hospitality and frankness of the Polynesians, but Louis was never greatly attracted to the area, so they set off for the archipelago of Samoa, crossing the equator as passengers in a trading schooner appropriately named *Equator*. Anxious now to secure a foothold in what seemed a paradise, they purchased in 1890 the estate of Vailima in the large island of Upolu, in Western Samoa. Like most of the archipelago the estate was mountainous and thickly afforested, with a tropical oceanic climate, tempered and copiously watered by breezes from the sea. In a letter of 13 July 1890, Stevenson wrote to a friend, 'The ancestral acres run to upwards of three hundred and enjoy the ministrations of five streams, hence the name.' But the name Vailima had probably been suggested to him by an early memory of a Highland holiday in Kingussie in Strathspey when, from the house named Greenfields in Spey Road, he had been deeply impressed, when looking across to the magnificent mountains on the other side of the valley, by five torrents, foaming white after rain, which converged to form a thundering cascade as they joined the Spey.

The Stevenson family on the *Equator* as she leaves Honolulu for the South Sea Islands in 1889

Unknown to the purchaser, however, the Vailima area had a sinister reputation. It was the site of an ancient fort which a bloody tribal battle had made *tabu*, a place haunted forever by the *aitu* or ghosts of the slain. A contractor was engaged to build a house on the lower slopes of Mount Vaea, which is densely covered by coconut palms, breadfruit, hibiscus and tree ferns, with tropical undergrowth. The estate was of four hundred acres, but only a small part could be cultivated, owing to the uneven surface and rapid growth of vegetation. A small

The great writer's last home: the house at Vailima, painted by Count Pieri Nerli in 1892, prior to the addition of the large hall in the same year

bungalow was first erected to accommodate the builders, and it was in this restricted space that the family, joined by Margaret Stevenson, Louis's mother, made their home until a larger house was built later in 1891.

The Samoans were a tall, handsome, ingenuous people, not prone to the imported diseases from Europe that took a fearful toll of many of the other islanders. They had formerly practised wars, but not human sacrifices or cannibalism. They had been converted to Christianity by various denominations, which Stevenson rather frowned on, because of the unnecessary rituals which displaced the native beliefs. The charity of the missionaries, especially towards lepers, was something he approved of, and on his visits to the leper community he refused to wear the customary gloves, to avoid offending the sufferers. When the Stevensons arrived, a rivalry between claimants to the kingship had led to a renewal of tribal wars, and for most of the remaining five years of Stevenson's life, the war drums throbbed in the surrounding jungle. But he was not perturbed. He continued his literary work in the knowledge that his person was sacred, as he had many friends on both sides, and Vailima was *tabu*.

Tusitala, Protector of the Samoans

Over and above the tribal friction, to Stevenson's anger and fierce protest, there was a 'satanical' presence known as colonialism. The year before his arrival, in far-off Berlin, a conference between Britain, Germany and the United States had been held to share out Samoa, no Samoans being invited or consulted. The chivalrous Louis took up the cudgels on behalf of his friends, and formed an alliance with Mataafa, one of the royal rivals, whose claim to the kingship of Samoa was being strongly supported by the Roman Catholic Bishop. Mataafa, according to one who knew both him and Stevenson, was a handsome charming man, a sort of South Seas Rob Roy, as wise as courageous. In short, he was Stevenson's ideal hero, in defence of whom Louis wrote letters to the London *Times*, exposing the political chicanery in Samoa. It was far from being a paradise. The chief town of Upolu was the seaport and naval base of Apia, some miles from Vailima. Such was its reputation for all kinds of vice that it was known as the 'hell of the Pacific'. Sailors, merchants, speculators, tourists and the flotsam of humanity of all races contributed to its bad reputation, though this was to some extent alleviated by the presence of missionaries, doctors and administrators. Of the missionaries, the closest friend of the Stevensons was James Chalmers, a dedicated and highly principled Scotsman, who left for New Guinea to convert the inland tribes and was killed and eaten by cannibals nine years later.

The house at Vailima after completion, from the book by Laurie Stubbs, *Stevenson's Shrine: the record of a pilgrimage* (1903)

Meantime, by 1891, the new house was completed, with offices and gardens. After initial misfits, whom Fanny sent packing, a large staff of Samoan servants was engaged, happy to work for a kind and sympathetic master. Fanny enthusiastically supervised, with such authority that she was credited with supernatural powers, as also was Louis, who was given the native title of Tusitala, teller of tales. Such was the power of his presence that until recent years there were Samoans who swore they saw the *aitu* of Tusitala at Vailima. His involvement in local politics used up much of his mental and physical energy. Vailima in fact became a thorn in the flesh for the politicians. After one violent exchange of accusations, he was nearly deported, but he persevered and published his protests under the title *A Footnote to History*. This caused such consternation that two of the most obnoxious German tyrants were dismissed. With great glee Stevenson heard that copies of his book, in a German translation, had been burned publicly in Berlin. He was a demigod in Samoa, and to show their gratitude for arranging their release from prison, a large band laboured to build a fine road to Vailima, naming it 'The Road of the Loving Heart'.

A feast held by Stevenson on the verandah at Vailima to celebrate completion of 'The Road of the Loving Heart'

The Europeans and the Americans regarded him as a maverick. When he lightheartedly engaged in a paperchase on a Sunday he was forced to apologise in public for his 'relapse into barbarism'. He forecast what fate was in store for Samoa and his own house. Even as early as 1891, the house not yet roofed, he wrote in irony, 'It will be a fine legacy to the Imperial German Majesty's protectorate and doubtless the Governor will take it for his country house'. He had second sight: in 1905, it became the residence of the German Governor.

Stevenson paid several visits to Australia from Samoa during his last four years, for various personal reasons: legal, business and perhaps for the pleasure of a sea voyage. He resided chiefly at the Union Club, Sydney, where a small museum of his possessions is still on view.

The Stevenson family and household photographed by J. Davis on 31 July 1892, two years before R. L. S.'s death. On the verandah are Joe D. Strong (Belle's husband), Mrs Margaret Stevenson, Lloyd Osbourne, R. L. S., Fanny Stevenson, Lafaele (cattleman); centre row, Mary (maid), Talojo (cook), Austin Strong, Belle Strong (Fanny's daughter) and (with axe) Tomasi (assistant cook); front row, Savea (plantation boy), Elena (laundress) and Arrick (pantry boy)

An Unyielding Spirit

The five years at Vailima, despite these unforeseen annoyances, were productive, even though he often suffered from writer's cramp and was sometimes so debilitated that, unable to speak, in dictating *St Ives* and *Weir of Hermiston* (both left unfinished) he had to communicate with his stepdaughter Belle by deaf-and-dumb alphabet, learned for this purpose. Yet he wrote several South Sea stories, *The Beach of Falesa*, *Island Nights' Entertainments*, *The Ebb-tide*, and *The Wrecker*, the latter two in collusion with Lloyd Osbourne.

But there is no doubt that, even half a world distant, the Scottish scene was where he was completely at ease, at his most masterful. The only exception, where he had not felt happy with the result, was *St Ives*, a romance of the Napoleonic prisoners-of-war held in Edinburgh and the Pentlands. Written under the stress of extreme physical weakness, it is the triumph of a spirit that would not yield.

Throughout the autumn of 1894 he had a fresh access of power, and resumed work on what he first called *The Justice Clerk*, a long-contemplated novel based on the conflict of father and son. The father figure was built convincingly round Robert MacQueen, Lord Braxfield, notorious in the 1790s for his savage and jeering manner on the bench. The son was the only child of a subservient wife, scion of a distinguished family. The comparison with Stevenson's own case can hardly be avoided. At last, in his dying months, he achieved the complete mastery of both Scots and English, with a sinewy prose that he had been aiming at all his life, with no extraneous ornaments. Although he wrote only half of the projected novel, he sketched the plot to its happy conclusion. So in *Weir of Hermiston*, we are not left dissatisfied by an unfinished tale.

His genius had all miraculously come to fruition when, like a thunderclap out of a serene sky, he was struck down instantly by a cerebral haemorrhage, on the evening of 3 December 1894. The news, when it reached Britain, was received with shocked disbelief.

R. L. S., now too weak to hold a pen, dictating the text of *Weir of Hermiston* to his stepdaughter Belle

The last photograph taken of R. L. S., in 1894

Requiem

The Samoans gathered from all parts to pay homage to the true friend of an exploited and abused people. Forty mourning warriors hewed a path through the forest to the summit of Mount Vaea, where Stevenson had wished to be buried. The following day, with great difficulty, his coffin was carried up the fresh trail to the grave. His tomb of massive concrete blocks, in the Samoan manner, was a work of great labour, carried out expeditiously.

On either side is a bronze plate, one bearing the inscription in Samoan, 'The Tomb of Tusitala', with an appropriate quotation from the Samoan Bible of the speech of Ruth to Naomi, 'Whither thou goest, I will go; and where thou lodgest, I will lodge; thy people shall be my people, and thy God my God. Where thou diest I will die, and there will I be buried.' The plate is bordered by a thistle and a hibiscus. In a panel, in English, is his famous *Requiem*, written ten years before. There is also a large bas-relief of Stevenson on his couch (cast in America in 1887 by Saint-Gaudens, the famous American sculptor) near the foot of Mount Vaea.

His mother had spent the last three years at Vailima and was at his deathbed to console Fanny, a task that was beyond her. Her own private feelings may well have been of gratitude, that her own love, Cummy's and Fanny's and the love of Louis's many friends, had been so richly repaid in his wonderful works.

The key to Stevenson's miraculous life work undoubtedly is to be found in his unique pervasive philosophy. He was always on the look-out for something unusually fortunate happening to him. And naturally, when it occurred, he recognised it as a gift from Heaven, and not only acknowledged it with gratitude, but put it to the best use. Such an unquenchable optimist can never fail to be an inspiration to humanity.

Stevenson's tomb at the summit of Mount Vaea, showing the biblical inscription in the Samoan language

To S. R. Crockett

BLOWS the wind today, and the sun and the rain are flying,
Blows the wind on the moors today and now,
Where about the graves of the martyrs the whaups are crying,
My heart remembers how!

Grey recumbent tombs of the dead in desert places,
Standing stones on the vacant wine-red moor,
Hills of sheep, and the howes of the silent vanished races,
And winds, austere and pure:

Be it granted to me to behold you again in dying,
Hills of home! and to hear again the call;
Hear about the graves of the martyrs the peewees crying,
And hear no more at all.

The tropics vanish.
(a view of Edinburgh from Swanston)

THE tropics vanish, and meseems that I,
From Halkerside, from topmost Allermuir,
Or steep Caerketton, dreaming gaze again.
Far set in fields and woods, the town I see
Spring gallant from the shallows of her smoke,
Cragged, spired, and turreted, her virgin fort
Beflagged. About, on seaward drooping hills,
New folds of city glitter. Last, the Forth
Wheels ample waters set with sacred isles,
And populous Fife smokes with a score of towns.

Over the Sea to Skye

Chorus
Sing me a song of a lad that is gone,
Say, could that lad be I?
Merry of soul he sailed on a day
Over the sea to Skye.

MULL was astern, Rum on the port,
Eigg on the starboard bow:
Glory of youth glowed in his soul:
Where is that glory now?

Chorus

Give me again all that was there,
Give me the sun that shone!
Give me the eyes, give me the soul,
Give me the lad that's gone!

Chorus

Billow and breeze, islands and seas,
Mountains of rain and sun,
All that was good, all that was fair,
All that is me is gone.

Chorus

A Camp
(from *Travels with a Donkey*)

THE bed was made, the room was fit,
By punctual eve the stars were lit;
The air was still, the water ran,
No need was there for maid or man,
When we put up, my ass and I,
At God's green caravanserai.

The Vagabond

GIVE to me the life I love,
Let the lave go by me,
Give the jolly heaven above
And the byway nigh me.
Bed in the bush with stars to see,
Bread I dip in the river –
There's the life for a man like me,
There's the life for ever.

Let the blow fall soon or late,
Let what will be o'er me;
Give the face of earth around
And the road before me.
Wealth I seek not, hope nor love,
Nor a friend to know me;
All I seek, the heaven above
And the road below me.

Or let the autumn fall on me
Where afield I linger,
Silencing the bird on tree,
Biting the blue finger.
White as meal the frosty field –
Warm the fireside haven –
Not to autumn will I yield,
Not to winter even.

Let the blow fall soon or late,
Let what will be o'er me;
Give the face of earth around,
And the road before me.
Wealth I ask not, hope nor love,
Nor a friend to know me;
All I ask, the heaven above
And the road below me.

I have trod...

I HAVE trod the upward and the downward slope;
I have endured and done in days before;
I have longed for all, and bid farewell to hope;
I have lived and loved, and closed the door.

The Celestial Surgeon

IF I have faltered more or less
In my great task of happiness;
If I have moved among my race
And shown no glorious morning face;
If beams from happy human eyes
Have moved me not; if morning skies
Books, and my food, and morning rain
Knocked on my sullen heart in vain –
Lord, thy most pointed pleasure take
And stab my spirit broad awake;
Or Lord, if too obdurate I,
Choose thou, before that spirit die,
A piercing pain, a killing sin,
And to my dead heart run them in!

The Lamplighter
(from *A Child's Garden of Verses*)

MY TEA is nearly ready and the sun has left the sky;
It's time to take the window to see Leerie going by;
For every night at teatime and before you take your seat,
With lantern and with ladder he goes posting up the street.

Now Tom would be a drover and Maria go to sea,
And my papa's a banker and as rich as he can be;
But I, when I am stronger and can choose what I'm to do,
O, Leerie, I'll go round at night and light the lamps with you.

For we are very lucky with a lamp before the door,
And Leerie stops to light it as he lights so many more;
But O! before you hurry by with ladder and with light,
O Leerie, see a little child and nod to him tonight!

Memorial to R. L. S. in St Giles' Cathedral, Edinburgh

IMPORTANT DATES IN STEVENSON'S LIFE

Acknowledgements
Edinburgh Academy, p. 1; Edinburgh City Libraries, pp. 12, 14; Lady Dunpark, pp. 2, 7 (right), 8 (top left), 11 (left), 16 (left), 19 (top), 20, 21 (right), 23 (top), 26, 27 (top), 28 (left); Lady Stairs Museum, Edinburgh, pp. 3, 4 (left), 5, 7 (left), 8 (top right), 15, 18 (right), 19 (bottom), 21 (left), 23 (bottom), 24, 25, 27 (bottom), 28 (right), 29, back cover; Scottish National Portrait Gallery, front cover, pp. 4 (right), 13, 16 (right).

Text by Forbes Macgregor, BA
ISBN 0-7117-0320-5
© 1989 Jarrold Colour Publications
Printed in Great Britain by Jarrold and Sons Ltd, Norwich. 189